Let's Find Out

Dinosaur Explorer

Dougal Dixon

First published in the UK in 2014 by:
QED Publishing
A Quarto Group Company
The Old Brewery
6 Blundell Street
London N7 9BH

www.qed-publishing.co.uk

Designed by Melissa Alaverdy

A catalogue record for this book is
available from the British Library.

ISBN 978 1 78171 546 8

Printed in China

Picture credits
(fc=front cover)

Martin Knowelden 1, 2, 4-5, 6, 7, 8-9, 10-11,
12-13, 14-15, 16-17, 20, 21, 22, 23, 24

Shutterstock fc Ozja, 2-3 Milagli,
18-19 Computer Earth

Contents

The world in the past

Animals from the past did not look like animals today. Some looked very strange.

Some of the strangest of these animals were the **dinosaurs**.

Tyrannosaurus

You are lucky that you do not live in those days.

Tyrannosaurus was a big, **fierce** dinosaur. It could have swallowed you whole!

It was larger than an elephant. It could eat other dinosaurs.

Gallimimus

Gallimimus looked
a bit like an ostrich.

It ran around the plains.

It had long
fingers on
short front legs.

It had long back legs
to run away from
fierce meat eaters.

Diplodocus

Diplodocus was one of the biggest dinosaurs.

It was the size of a house. It had a tiny head on a long neck.

Diplodocus ate leaves
and twigs. It spent
all its time eating.

Ouranosaurus

Ouranosaurus was a big dinosaur that ate plants.

It had a long snout and a wide mouth.

It had a brightly coloured **sail** on its back. It might have used it to signal to other dinosaurs.

Sail

Stegosaurus

Stegosaurus had hard plates in two rows on its back. It had spikes at the end of its tail.

spikes

Its tiny **brain** was
the size of a walnut.

It had small teeth
for eating plants.

plates

Triceratops

Triceratops had three horns on its head.

It ate plants, and used its horns to fight off meat eaters like Tyrannosaurus.

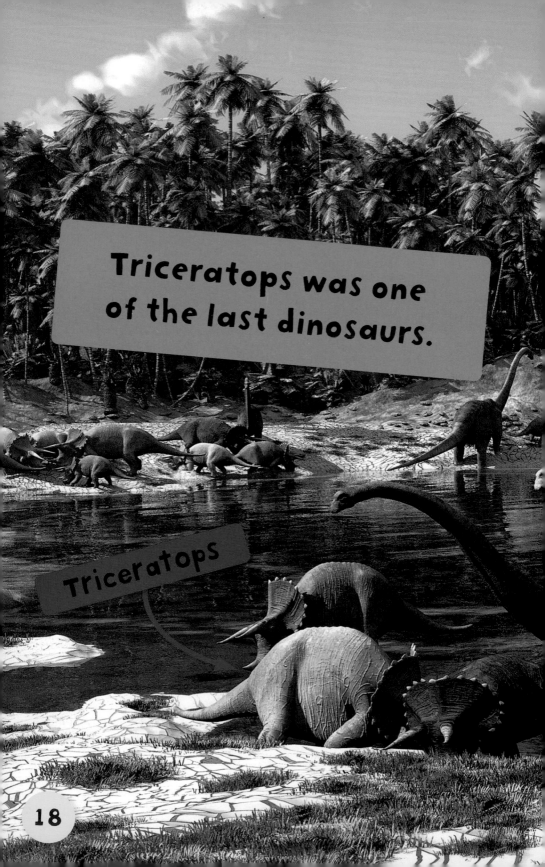

Triceratops was one of the last dinosaurs.

Triceratops

All dinosaurs are now **extinct.**

What do you think?

Which dinosaur was very fierce?

Which dinosaur was as big as a house?

Can you name two dinosaurs that start with a 'T'?

Which dinosaur had a coloured sail on its back?

Why did Gallimimus need long legs?

Which dinosaur had three horns on its head?

Did dinosaurs have longer legs at the front or the back?

Glossary

brain   the part of the head that people and animals use to think

dinosaur   a type of animal that lived a long time ago

extinct   when a type of animal has died out

fierce   scary and dangerous

sail   a big fin made of bones and covered in skin